Creative Ideas
for
Library Media Center
Facilities

CREATIVE IDEAS FOR FOR LIBRARY MEDIA CENTER FACILITIES

THOMAS L. HART
Professor, Florida State University

1990
LIBRARIES UNLIMITED, INC.
Englewood, Colorado

LIBRARIES UNLIMITED, INC.
P.O. Box 3988
Englewood, Colorado 80155-3988

Library of Congress Cataloging-in-Publication Data

Hart, Thomas L.
   Creative ideas for library media center facilities / Thomas L. Hart.
     ix, 75 p. 22x28 cm.
     Includes bibliographical references.
     ISBN 0-87287-736-1.
     1. School libraries--Activity programs. 2. Media programs (Education) I. Title.
Z675.S3H267   1990
027.8'223--dc20
                                       90-5437
                                          CIP

Contents

Preface

Roberta Mann, the library media specialist at Oak Ridge Elementary School in Tallahassee, and Wessie Connell, the library director for the Grady County Public Library in Cairo, Georgia, provided the inspiration for this book.

Roberta Mann shared with me ideas from a Florida Association for Media in Education (FAME) convention, which she was able to implement successfully in her library media center, constructing a multimedia "train" as a focal point. Wessie Connell obtained a grant to convert an old school bus into a multimedia center for children.

These projects illustrate the importance of creative activities in school and public libraries. Observing the success of these two projects, I was motivated to identify other creative projects from all over the United States and present them in a book.

The proposal for this book was sent to several publishers. Dr. David Loertscher of Libraries Unlimited enthusiastically welcomed the possibility of publishing a book in the school library media field with black-and-white and color plates.

This book is planned as the first of a series to share the most innovative ideas from the school library media community. If you have creative activities you wish to contribute, please contact me.

Dr. Thomas L. Hart
School of Library and Information Studies
Florida State University
Tallahassee, Florida 32306
(904) 644-5775

THE LEARNING ENVIRONMENT

1

Imaginative Environments Form Lives and Build Characters

An imaginative learning environment can assist in creating lifelong memories. Memories associated with special occasions or environments remain sharp and clear to me even today.

When I was younger, my family told me about trips to a wonderful amusement park where there were swan boats in beautiful lagoons and a carousel with a brass ring. I always dreamed of catching the brass ring, which would allow me a free ride and another chance to catch the ring.

I still remember how, in the first grade, I did my spelling words using a canning jar full of letters on individual squares of thin cardboard. This was during World War II, and I later learned that we did this because paper was scarce. The classroom was drafty and dreary, but there was a wonderful coat closet where we dreamed up plays and created props from old curtains and boxes. And, along with a large aquarium and terrarium in the room was a special library corner.

I especially remember completing my first academic project, a fifth-grade paper on South America (complete with carefully traced maps), and one significant high school project, an eighty-page research paper on the Civil War.

Many other significant events and environments shaped my life: high school band, 4-H, junior and senior plays, church camp, good books and films, and family gatherings. Events that create vivid memories are important in forming our lives and characters.

The first section of this book is a summary of research in the fields of education, environmental psychology, and design concerning the impact of combinations of colors and lighting and other aspects of the environment on the educational enterprise.

In the second section, innovative projects from schools throughout the country are described and illustrated with photographs. The projects are arranged in related groups, such as special area features, displays, and reading incentive programs.

My attention was first drawn to creative school library media projects by the activities of Roberta Mann when she was the library media specialist at Oak Ridge Elementary School in Tallahassee, Florida.

Roberta attended a session at a Florida Association for Media in Education (FAME) convention where plans were distributed for a "train" consisting of several multimedia carrels. Her library media center was large, with bland furniture and black metal shelving, and Roberta felt it needed something to unify it and provide a focal point. She presented the multimedia train idea to the principal and the executive board of the PTA who readily gave their support. A member of the board who was a draftsman offered to prepare blueprints. The PTA paid for the construction costs, and a local high school industrial arts class built the train as their spring project. Teachers and parents painted the train. By the time it was completed and put in place, the train had become the focal point not only of the library media center, but of the entire school. Students earned time to use the activity centers in the carrels through good behavior in the classroom and elsewhere in the school.

When Roberta Mann moved to a new school, Killearn Lakes Elementary, she planned another type of focal point—a double-decker bus. This project is explained in detail in the second section of this book.

The Grady County Public Library in Cairo, Georgia, needed more space in their children's area. The library director, Miss Wessie Connell, devised a plan to make a "Secret Place" media center for the children. When the grant proposal was funded, the public library turned an old school bus into a wonderful outdoor multimedia center. Local businessmen provided electric lights and outlets, screens, and carpeting. The high school art class painted the bus and designed enlarged drawings of fairy tale characters for interior decorations. The vocational arts department of the high school built tables and seats for the bus, which was located in the shade of magnolia trees on the grounds of the library.

Other creative projects, as exciting and successful as these, are described in detail in this book.

2

The Impact of the Environment on the Educational Process

Research has demonstrated that our surroundings have a great deal to do with the development of our intellectual powers and personality patterns. The environment and our perception of it together have the greatest impact on our minds.

THE ENVIRONMENT AND ITS EFFECTS ON LEARNING

Several publications have addressed issues concerning school library media center environments. Estelle Jussim makes a plea for "the psychobiological needs of idiosyncratic individuals" in an article where she states, "That most crucial factor in the design of interior spaces—*the physical and psychological characteristics of ordinary mortals*—is left to the mercy of obsolete building laws, the hangovers of nineteenth-century linear mentality, or the blithely destructive ignorance of the everyday contractor."[1] Philip Bennett's planning manual, *Creating a Library Environment for Learning*, runs the gamut of design criteria for children.[2] Almost all of it is applicable to all types of libraries. Extracts of this manual may be found in Bennett's *Wisconsin Library Bulletin* article on the physiological, psychological, and sociological design factors for users.[3]

Other recent publications, most focussing upon school environments, have also examined environmental design implications for children. A special issue of *Children in Contemporary Society* entitled "Environmental Design for Young Children" contains seventeen brief articles dealing with both theoretical and practical concerns.[4] Another special issue, from *School Review*, August 1974, entitled "Learning Environments," is a compendium of information for use in designs for children and has since been published as a monograph.[5]

A planning manual for libraries of all types is *Behavioral Space Planning and Practical Design for Libraries*. Developed from a series of seminars conducted by Aaron and Elaine Cohen, this workbook covers many aspects of library interior planning from the point of view of an architect or interior designer. It also covers, as the title implies, the behavioral aspects of library design in a manner not usually found in planning literature.[6]

The most significant research concerning satisfactory study environments has been guided by Robert Sommer. Beginning in 1968, he examined study behavior wherever it happened to occur. "The goal of this research was to learn the conditions that make for a satisfying study environment in the hopes of feeding this information back to the people who design educational spaces," he states in his first book.[7] For this reason, he made a number of papers and related materials from this research project available to architects, designers, and planners.[8]

Sommer's monographs contain additional useful material. His 1969 work, *Personal Space: The Behavioral Basis of Design*, not only contains most of his research concerning libraries, but also presents his theories and observations on humans and artificial environments.[9] His later book, *Tight Spaces: Hard Architecture and How To Humanize It*, continues the themes of the previous volume by looking at the effects of institutional architecture on people.[10]

A fourth book by Sommer, *Design Awareness*, concentrates on "methods of developing environmental awareness and on the consequences of this awareness in regard to user-generated and user-maintained systems."[11] Although not written specifically for library media centers, this work is useful in helping library media specialists to become sensitive to the artificial environments they help to build and maintain. Chapter 10 of *Design Awareness* is of special value, dealing with post-construction building evaluations.

ENVIRONMENTAL DESIGN

Although much of the information in this section does not precisely emphasize library planning, the themes of environmental psychology, behavior and environment, and human engineering are as applicable to libraries as to any other artificial environment affecting people's behavior and activities.

The conceptual framework of environmental design has been established by a number of authors working in various disciplines. David Canter in *Psychology for Architects* makes a case for the application of psychological research to architectural planning. The contributions of psychology, he says, can be made at the three stages of building design: conception, specification, and evaluation.[12] John Zeisel covers a similar area from a sociological perspective in his book *Sociology and Architectural Design*,[13] as does Robert Gutman in his article "Architecture and Sociology."[14] Richard Dober's 1969 volume, *Environmental Design*, although "biased toward the urban situation" applies to smaller settings as well. The objective, he says, is "to make human habitation as varied, enjoyable, stimulating, healthy, and rewarding as possible."[15]

An earlier article by Raymond Studer and David Stea is entitled "Architectural Programming, Environmental Design, and Human Behavior." The authors discuss the impact of human biological and psychological systems on architecture: The environmental designer's task is to bring the designed environment into equilibrium with those human systems; "architectural" form, structure, and space, no longer considered ends in themselves, become the means that may be employed to establish this equilibrium.[16]

In a small monograph, John Harrigan has attempted to provide some practical information to architects on the application of behavioral and human factors to architectural programs. While the creation of physical settings sensitive to users' needs has always been a primary goal of design, the behavioral science and human factors disciplines have now developed principles and practices that markedly improve the likelihood that design concepts will lead to suitable environments.[17] Harrigan's study provides a classification of considerations "which comprise the suggested points of linkage between the behavioral sciences and human factors disciplines and the architectural program."[18]

Writing from an architectural point of view, other authors make contributions to environmental design theory. Geoffrey Broadbent, head of the School of Architecture, Portsmouth Polytechnic, England, presents a treatise about the relevance of human sciences to the architecture profession.[19] Robert Bechtel, in his book *Enclosing Behavior*, argues that the design professions should consider behavior above form. This is a book with a single message: There is no such thing as the design of space or spaces. "*Behavior*, not space, is enclosed by architecture."[20] This is reemphasized in *Behavioral Architecture: Toward an Accountable Design Process*.[21]

C. M. Deasy, a California architect, in his book *Design for Human Affairs*, presents a thorough commentary on the implications of and the necessity for sociological-psychological based design. His philosophy is that buildings are devices that should make people more effective in whatever activity they pursue.

It is apparent that the designer who is seriously concerned with the question of human effectiveness must widen the scope of his interest to include a complex new set of human factors. If personal motivation and group interaction are elements that affect our competence as human beings, the designer has a clear responsibility to create environments that will do as much as an environment can do to recognize and accommodate these factors.[22]

Deasy goes on to discuss the problems architects have in using this new environmental design information, but he also argues that the design profession must make use of it because the "purpose of planning or design is not to create a physical artifact, but a setting for human behavior.... Designers will require a new mindset that will recognize that it is human behavior that is rational and that the structure that does not accommodate it is irrational."[23]

ENVIRONMENTAL PSYCHOLOGY

A number of works deal specifically with environmental psychology, a field closely related to environmental design. Joachim Wohlwill presents historical background and points to some probable directions in his article "The Emerging Discipline of Environmental Psychology."[24] Two review articles in the *Annual Review of Psychology* point to the expansion of this relatively new field.

The first, by Kenneth Craik, published in 1973, cites 280 items in its bibliography.[25] Daniel Stokols wrote the second review, published five years later. This time the literature citations had increased to 497, with no overlap from the first review.

At a time when environmentalists and economists are proclaiming that "small is beautiful," the research literature on human behavior in relation to its environmental settings continues to expand at a staggering rate.... Though it is a simple matter to chart the quantitative growth of environmental psychology over the past 5 years, an assessment of the scientific quality and coherence of this area is considerably more difficult. A major complexity in this regard is that the boundaries of the field are not easily delimited. The study of human behavior in relation to the environment, broadly speaking, would seem to encompass all areas within psychology, let alone most of the behavioral sciences.[26]

Among the major works in the field of environmental psychology are a number produced by authors associated with the Environmental Psychology Program at the City University of New York. In 1970, Harold Proshansky, William Ittelson, and Leanne Rivlin edited a collection of readings entitled *Environmental Psychology: Man and His Physical Setting.*[27] Considered to be a landmark in the development of this field, the work brought together for the first time many important writings from the various disciplines that were contributing to this new area of study.

In 1976, a second edition was published by the same authors. Titled *Environmental Psychology: People and Their Physical Settings*, this book of readings was designed as a companion to a 1974 textbook written by the same three authors, along with Gary Winkle.[28] The text was descriptively titled *An Introduction to Environmental Psychology.*[29]

Another collection of readings, this one with an architectural bias, was produced in 1972 by Robert Gutman. The aim of *People and Buildings* was "to urge both architects and behavioral scientists to recognize certain features of the phenomena to which their work is addressed."[30] Two years later another anthology was published, entitled *Designing for Human Behavior: Architecture and the Behavioral Sciences*. This work, which "attempts to synthesize and digest recent changes in architectural philosophy which are concomitant with the development of the field of environmental psychology," is a volume of the Community Development Series of Dowden,

Hutchinson, and Ross.[31] Other issues in this series are also valuable, such as *Behavioral Research Methods in Environmental Design*. This is a collection of papers meant

> to indicate to the environmental designer the usefulness and characteristics of selected social science techniques for some of his ongoing problems, and to indicate to the social scientist a rich lode of context, ready and waiting to serve as a literal new world of application for techniques at his command.[32]

David Canter has produced two collections of pertinent readings. With Terrence Lee, he edited *Psychology and the Built Environment* in 1974.[33] In 1975, with Peter Stringer, he published a work entitled *Environmental Interaction: Psychological Approaches to Our Built Environment*. This second title contains a small subchapter devoted to the spatial environment of the library.[34]

Several recent publications round out the sampling of environmental psychology literature. Irwin Altman and Joachim Wohlwill have compiled the first two volumes in a series entitled *Human Behavior and Environment: Advances in Theory and Research*. These are "based on the assumption that research has proceeded to the point where it is useful to initiate the process of integration of knowledge about selected environmental and behavioral topics."[35] Daniel Stokols has aimed in a similar direction with his volume *Perspectives on Environment and Behavior: Theory, Research, and Applications*.[36]

ERGONOMICS
AND HUMAN FACTORS

Another aspect of environmental design is ergonomics, or human factor engineering, which is concerned with the human body and its relationship to equipment and physical facilities. David Meister's *Human Factors: Theory and Practice*[37] and Ernest J. McCormick's *Human Factors in Engineering and Design*[38] provide detailed coverage of this field.

A layman's introduction that provides a considerable amount of information applicable to libraries, by Corwin Bennett, is *Spaces for People: Human Factors in Design*.[39] It emphasizes the ergonomic considerations that relate to the anatomical and physiological aspects of humans and the application of these considerations to building design. An earlier application of these concepts to libraries was made by Francis McCarthy. Using the term "human mechanics," he related body dimensions to the proper spacing and size of library equipment.[40] McCarthy's measurements and figures are used in DeChiara and Callender's architectural reference book entitled *Time-Saver Standards for Building Types*.[41]

M. M. Ayoub's article "Work Place Design and Posture" provides recommendations and guidelines for office workers. This, of course, also has application for libraries as they are, indeed, work places. Ayoub asserts that comfort, physical well-being, and output are greatly influenced by the degree to which physical facilities fit the worker population. To design spaces to fit the operator population properly, the relevant anthropometric, biomechanical, physiological, anatomical, and operating characteristics of humans must be considered at the initial stages of design.[42]

Using similar criteria, Galitz and Laska gathered data on the behavior and work habits of computer personnel.[43] As libraries rely more and more on computers this type of information will become more applicable.

EFFECTS OF COLOR

There have been several studies of color and its effect on people and their behavior. Gerard, who examined the effect of colored lights on psychophysiological functions, found blue light produced relaxed behavior and red illumination was associated with tension and excitement.[44] Aaronson reported much the same results.[45] Plack and Shick reviewed an extensive amount of literature and found that color affected changes in mood and emotional state, psychomotor performance, muscular activity, rate of breathing, pulse rate, and blood pressure.[46]

Hanlon referred to several studies and concluded that people tend to feel warmer in rooms decorated with reds, yellows, oranges, and rich browns and in rooms with low ceilings and warm incandescent lighting.[47] Conversely, people feel cooler when rooms are decorated in blues, greens, pale neutrals, and white and when the lighting is fluorescent. In Faily, Bursor, and Musemeche's research review, Garnsey reported that a salmon-gray bank office was perceived to be too warm.[48] The heat problem was reduced by simply changing the color of the interior to a light blue-gray-green and painting the interior columns white. They also concluded that Notre Dame coach Knute Rockne must have believed that colors affect the moods of people. It is reported that he had his home team locker rooms painted a high-energy red and the locker rooms of the visiting team painted a restful blue.

EFFECTS OF LIGHT

Artificial light sources do not accurately reproduce the full spectrum of sunlight. Incandescent lights are rich in red and yellow light but emit relatively little blue or green light. Cool-white fluorescent lights emit most of their radiant energy in the green and yellow bands of the spectrum. Eyes are most sensitive to light in this range. Full-spectrum fluorescent lights emit a significant portion of their radiant energy in the blue area of the spectrum; a small percentage of their radiant energy may fall into the ultraviolet (UV) range. Because the eye is less sensitive to blue light than to green and yellow light, rooms lit with full-spectrum fluorescent lights are often perceived as being dimly lit.

Zamkova and Krivitskaya augmented regular fluorescent light with ultraviolet suntan lamps in a controlled experiment involving schoolchildren.[49] When compared to the control group, students who received exposure to ultraviolet light showed increased levels of working ability, greater resistance to fatigue, improved academic performance, improved stability of clear vision, and increased weight and growth.

Richard Wurtman concluded that light has biological effects that are important to health and that some of these effects could be easily reproduced and measured in the experimental laboratory.[50] These effects were of two kinds: those that modify an individual's endocrine, hormone, and metabolic state by means of light reaching the retina; and those that resulted from light on the skin (e.g., vitamin D production, skin tanning, and dissociation of bilirubin). Wurtman also linked the kind and amount of light entering the eye with responses of the pineal gland and secretion of the hormone melatonin.[51] Melatonin, in turn, influences the functions of other glands, possibly as a result of direct action on specific areas of the brain.

Wurtman and Weisel studied the effects of light from cool-white lamps and full-spectrum Vita-Lite lamps on a group of rats. Their findings support the argument that environmental lighting has an effect on at least some neuro-endocrine functions.[52] Himmelfarb, Scott, and Thayer reported that light from Vita-Lite (full-spectrum) bulbs was significantly more effective in killing bacteria than light from standard cool-white bulbs.[53] Sharon, Feller, and Burney reported that golden hamsters exposed to full-spectrum bulbs (with a measurable UV output) had one-fifth as many tooth cavities as animals exposed to conventional fluorescent lights.[54] As well, gonad, submandibular gland, and total body weights were greater for animals raised under the simulated natural light (full-spectrum lights).

Maas, Jayson, and Kleiber reported studies comparing the effects of full-spectrum and cool-white light on a group of students at Cornell University.[55] The findings indicated that students studying under full-spectrum lights had the smallest decrease over time in critical flicker fusion (the frequency of intermittent stimulations of the eye at which flicker disappears) and an increase in visual acuity. Students studying under cool-white illumination demonstrated greater lethargy than those studying under full-spectrum lights.

Mayron, Ott, Nations, and Mayron also compared the effects of two different light sources on students.[56] One classroom was lit with conventional cool-white lights; the other classroom was lit with full-spectrum lights that had lead shields around the cathodes to eliminate the possibility of stray X-ray radiation. The authors observed a decrease in hyperactive behavior by students exposed to full-spectrum lighting.

Using time-lapse photography, Ott compared the effects of full-spectrum fluorescent lights to those of standard cool-white fluorescent lights on pupils.[57] These full-spectrum lights also had lead shields over the cathodes to prevent the radiation of suspected soft X-rays. It was concluded that the classroom behavior of the children showed dramatic improvement under shielded full-spectrum fluorescent lighting.

At the New York Academy of Science conference on the medical and biological effects of lighting held in November 1984, it was reported by Hathaway and Fiedler that light is a key to the general well-being of people confined to a physical facility a great portion of the day.[58] Wohlfarth completed a study in 1986, in Alberta, Canada, that determined that trace amounts of ultraviolet in classroom lighting significantly reduced the development of dental cavities and contributed to improved health.[59] There was an apparent enhanced sense of well-being and better attendance.

EFFECTS OF
LIGHTING AND COLOR
COMBINATIONS

A study by H. Wohlfarth and K. Sam of the effects of color and light variables on a small group of severely handicapped children and their teachers indicated that full-spectrum lighting in a classroom painted in relaxing shades of blue caused several measures to change significantly.[60] For example, the systolic blood pressure of the students (both blind and sighted) dropped approximately 20 points (from 120 to 100); aggressive behaviors dropped to 56 percent of normal levels; non-attentive behaviors dropped to approximately 23 percent of previous levels; and teachers reported that they found the environment much more relaxing and that they were able to have students complete more work.

A project designed to test a number of the variables identified in the literature was conducted under the auspices of Alberta Education between 1981 and 1985.[61] This project explored how classroom settings affect the well-being and performance of elementary schoolchildren and provides information that can be used to enhance the physical conditions in which teaching and learning take place. The study examined the effects of lighting, selected colors, and light/color combinations on students' activities and achievements, attitudes toward school subjects, misbehavior, absences due to illness, refractive eye problems, blood pressure, and mood variations; determined changes in the offtask behaviors of fifth-grade students caused by eliminating the electromagnetic and (possibly) stray ionizing radiation associated with fluorescent lighting; measured the effects of light/color combinations on the levels of noise in libraries; assessed the effect of supplemental ultraviolet light on the incidence of dental cavities and absences due to illness of fifth-grade students; and provided suggestions on cost-effective changes that can be made to classroom settings for the benefit of teachers and students.

Graves reported interesting results from another project in Alberta, Canada, in which four 700-student elementary schools were studied.[62] The findings reinforced well-documented color effects that include relaxation (cool colors), activity (warm colors), alertness (yellow/red), and strength variations (blue = strong, pink = weak). School I had the typical neutral color schemes with accents of bright colors and cool-white fluorescent lighting; school II had the same color scheme as school I with full-spectrum lighting; school III had a color scheme of blue, yellow, and neutral with cool-white fluorescent lighting; and school IV had the same color scheme as school III, but with full-spectrum lighting. The results were definitely in favor of the combination of the blue, yellow, and neutral color scheme and full-spectrum lighting.

CONCLUSIONS

Developing a creative learning environment is supported by person-environment theories that emphasize that behavior settings shape the behavior of people who inhabit them. When people have a congruent environmental relationship, this causes them to have stability, achievement, and satisfaction. Individuals are most satisfied and productive in an environment that moves them from their perceived self toward their ideal self-concept. All of these theories provide evidence for a colorful, interesting, creative place to learn with ambience.

The Environment and Its Effect on Learning

It is crucial that interior learning spaces meet the physical and psychological needs of their occupants. The space needs to be designed for children, young adults, or combinations of both. Many of the sources cited in this chapter provide concrete examples for creating a satisfactory study environment. There is a constant battle between economical, efficient space and how to humanize institutional space.

Environmental Design

Considerable research is available to support the needs of environmental psychology, behavior and environment, and human engineering. Human habitation areas must be varied, enjoyable, stimulating, healthy, and rewarding. The major purpose of planning or designing buildings is not to create a physical artifact, but rather to create a setting for human behavior.

Environmental Psychology

This is a relatively new area of research that emphasizes that the architect and or building designer has a responsibility to create environments that will assist humans in effectively using the spaces provided. This area emphasizes the study of human behavior in relation to environment.

Ergonomics and Human Factors

Research in this area emphasizes the human body and its relationship to equipment and physical facilities and measurements for utilizing the best furniture, seating, and equipment configurations for staff and users.

Effects of Color

A number of studies that support the concepts of where and how to use colors most effectively:

    a. Reds, yellows, oranges, and rich browns create a warm feeling with incandescent lighting.

    b. Blues, greens, pale neutrals, and white are cool feeling under fluorescent lighting.

Effects of Light

Considerable research has been recently reported concerning the effects of lighting on learning. It is essential for students to have at least minimal access to natural outdoor lighting for physical and intellectual well-being. Hyperactive behavior by students can be reduced through the use of full-spectrum fluorescent lighting versus cool-white fluorescent lighting.

Effects of Light and Color Combinations

The most significant study in this area reinforced well-documented color effects:

a. relaxation — cool colors

b. activity — warm colors

c. alertness — yellow/red colors

d. strong — blue

e. weak — pink

The results of this research favored blue, yellow, and neutral colors with full-spectrum lighting rather than fluorescent lighting.

NOTES

1. Estelle Jussim, "Personal Space and the Media Center," *School Media Quarterly* 2 (Spring 1974): 189.

2. Philip M. Bennett, *Creating a Library Environment for Learning* (Madison: University of Wisconsin, Department of Engineering and Applied Science, 1978). 89pp.

3. Philip M. Bennett, "Users Come First in Design: Physiological, Psychological, and Sociological Factors," *Wisconsin Library Bulletin* 74 (March-April 1978): 51-58.

4. Mary Frank, ed., "Environmental Design for Young Children," *Children in Contemporary Society* 11 (November 1977). ERIC ED 149 567. 52pp.

5. David G. Thomas, ed., *Learning Environments* (Chicago: University of Chicago Press, 1975). 233pp.

6. Aaron Cohen and Elaine Cohen, *Behavioral Space Planning and Practical Design for Libraries* (New York: Cohen, 1978). 200pp.

7. Robert Sommer, *The Ecology of Study Areas* (Davis: University of California, 1968), 6. ERIC ED 032 906.

8. Ibid., 53.

9. Robert Sommer, *Personal Space: The Behavioral Basis of Design* (Englewood Cliffs, N.J.: Prentice-Hall, 1969). 177pp.

10. Robert Sommer, *Tight Spaces: Hard Architecture and How To Humanize It* (Englewood Cliffs, N.J.: Prentice-Hall, 1974). 150pp.

11. Robert Sommer, *Design Awareness* (San Francisco: Reinhart, 1972), vi.

12. David V. Canter, *Psychology for Architects* (New York: John Wiley, 1974). 171pp.

13. John Zeisel, *Sociology and Architectural Design* (New York: Russell Sage Foundation, 1975). 57pp.

14. Robert Gutman, "Architecture and Sociology," *American Sociologist* 10 (November 1975): 219-228.

15. Richard P. Dober, *Environmental Design* (New York: Van Nostrand, 1969), preface.

16. Raymond G. Studer and David Stea, "Architectural Programming, Environmental Design, and Human Behavior," *Journal of Social Issues* 22 (January 1966): 127-136.

17. John E. Harrigan and Wesley S. Ward, *Human Factors Information Taxonomy: A Guide to User Oriented Architectural Services* (San Luis Obispo, Calif.: California Polytechnic State University, n.d.), 1.

18. John E. Harrigan, "Human Factors Information Taxonomy: Fundamental Human Factors Applications for Architectural Programs," *Human Factors* 16 (August 1974): 435.

19. Geoffrey Broadbent, *Design in Architecture: Architecture and the Human Sciences* (London: John Wiley, 1973). 504pp.

20. Robert B. Bechtel, *Enclosing Behavior* (Stroudsburg, Pa.: Dowden, Hutchinson, and Ross, 1977): ii.

21. Clovis Heimsath, *Behavioral Architecture: Toward an Accountable Design Process* (New York: McGraw-Hill, 1977). 203pp.

22. C. M. Deasy, *Design for Human Affairs* (Cambridge, Mass.: Schenkman, 1974), 14.

23. Ibid., 40.

24. Joachim F. Wohlwill, "The Emerging Discipline of Environmental Psychology," *American Psychologist* 25 (April 1970): 303-312.

25. Kenneth H. Craik, "Environmental Psychology," *Annual Review of Psychology* 24 (1973): 403-422.

26. Daniel Stokols, "Environmental Psychology," *Annual Review of Psychology* 29 (1978): 253-254.

27. Harold M. Proshansky, William H. Ittelson, and Leanne G. Rivlin, eds., *Environmental Psychology: Man and His Physical Setting* (New York: Holt, Rinehart, and Winston, 1970). 690pp.

28.   Harold M. Proshansky, William H. Ittelson, and Leanne G. Rivlin, eds., *Environmental Psychology: People and Their Physical Settings* (New York: Holt, Rinehart, and Winston, 1976). 632pp.

29.   William H. Ittelson et al., *An Introduction to Environmental Psychology* (New York: Holt, Rinehart, and Winston, 1974). 406pp.

30.   Robert Gutman, ed., *People and Buildings* (New York: Basic Books, 1972), xiv.

31.   Jon Lang et al., eds., *Designing for Human Behavior: Architecture and the Behavioral Sciences* (Stroudsburg, Pa.: Dowden, Hutchinson, and Ross, 1974), vii.

32.   William Michelson, ed., *Behavioral Research Methods in Environmental Design* (Stroudsburg, Pa.: Dowden, Hutchinson, and Ross, 1975), 1.

33.   David Canter and Terrence Lee, eds., *Psychology and the Built Environment* (New York: John Wiley, 1974). 213pp.

34.   David Canter and Cheryl Kenny, "The Spatial Environment," in *Environmental Interaction: Psychological Approaches to Our Physical Surroundings*, David Canter and Peter Stringer, eds. (New York: International Universities Press, 1975), 156-57.

35.   Irwin Altman and Joachim F. Wohlwill, eds., *Human Behavior and Environment: Advances in Theory and Research*, Volume 1 (New York: Plenum, 1976), vii.

36.   Daniel Stokols, ed., *Perspectives on Environment and Behavior: Theory, Research, and Applications* (New York: Plenum, 1977). 360pp.

37.   David Meister, *Human Factors: Theory and Practice* (New York: John Wiley, 1971). 415pp.

38.   Ernest J. McCormick, *Human Factors in Engineering and Design* (New York: McGraw-Hill, 1976). 491pp.

39.   Corwin Bennett, *Spaces for People: Human Factors in Design* (Englewood Cliffs, N.J.: Prentice-Hall, 1977). 195pp.

40.   Francis Joseph McCarthy, "Human Mechanics in Relation to Equipment," in *Planning Library Buildings for Service*, Harold L. Roth, ed. (Chicago: American Library Association, 1964), 27-37.

41.   Joseph DeChiara and John Hancock Callender, *Time-Saver Standards for Building Types* (New York: McGraw-Hill, 1973), 276-283.

42.   M. M. Ayoub, "Work Place Design and Posture," *Human Factors* 15 (June 1973): 265-268.

43.   Wilbert O. Galitz and Thomas J. Laska, "The Computer Operator and His Environment," *Human Factors* 12 (December 1970): 563-573.

44.   M. Gerard, "Differential Effects of Colored Lights on Psychophysiological Function," Ph.D. dissertation, University of California – Los Angeles, 1958. 301pp.

45.   B. S. Aaronson, "Colour Perception and Effect," *American Journal of Clinical Hypnosis* 14:1 (1971): 38-43.

46.   J. J. Plack and J. Shick, "The Effects of Colour on Human Behavior," *Association for the Study of Perception Journal* 9:1 (1974): 4-16.

47.   H. Hanlon, "A Learning, Working Environment," *Educational Horizons* 58:2 (1979): 89.

48.   A. Faily, D. E. Bursor, and R. A. Musemeche, "Research Review," *CEFP Journal* 175:5, 16-18.

49.   M. A. Zamkova and E. I. Krivitskaya, "Effect of Irradiation by Ultraviolet Erytheme Lamps on the Working Ability of School Children," *Gigiena i Sanitariia* 31, 41-44.

50.   Richard J. Wurtman, "Biological Implications of Artificial Illumination," paper presented at the National Technical Conference of the Illuminating Engineering Society, Phoenix, Arizona, 1968.

51.   Richard Wurtman, "The Pineal and Endocrine Function," *Hospital Practice*, 1986, 32-37.

52.   Richard J. Wurtman and J. H. Weisel, "Environmental Lighting and Neuroendocrine Function: Relationship between Spectrum of Light Source and Gonodal Growth," *Endocrinology* 85:6 (1969): 1218-1221.

53.   P. Himmelfarb, A. Scott, and P. S. Thayer, "Bactericidal Activity of a Broad-spectrum Illumination Source," *Applied Microbiology* (n.d.): 1013-1014.

54.   I. M. Sharon, R. P. Feller, and S. W. Burney, "The Effects of Lights of Different Spectra on Caries Incidence in the Golden Hamster," *Archives of Oral Biology* 19:12 (1971): 1417-1431.

55.   J. B. Maas, J. K. Jayson, and D. A. Kleiber, "Effects of Spectral Difference in Illumination on Fatigue," *Journal of Applied Psychology* 59:4 (1974): 524-26; and J. B. Maas et al., "Quality of Light Is Important—Not Just Quantity," *American School and University* 46:12 (1974): 31.

56.   L. W. Mayron, J. Ott, R. Nations, and E. L. Mayron, "Light Radiation and Academic Behavior," *Academy Therapy* 10:1 (1975): 34-47.

57.   J. Ott, "Influence of Fluorescent Lights on Hyperactivity and Learning Disabilities," *Journal of Learning Disabilities* 9:7 (1976): 22-27.

58.   W. E. Hathaway and D. R. Fiedler, "A Window on the Future: A View of Education and Educational Facilities," in *CEFP Journal* 25:2 (March-April 1987): 4-17.

59.   H. Wohlfarth, *Color and Light Effects on Students, Achievement, Behavior and Physiology* (Edmonton, Alberta: Planning Services Branch, Alberta Education, 1986). 182pp.

60.   H. Wohlfarth and K. Sam, *The Effects of Colour Psychodynamic Environment Modification upon Psycho-physiological and Behavioral Reactions of Severely Handicapped Children* (Edmonton, Alberta: Planning Services Branch, Alberta Education, 1981). 57pp.

61.   Ibid.

62.   B. Graves, "Facility Planning: Shedding Light on Learning," *American School and University* 57:7 (March 1985): 88-90.

PROJECTS
How to Spiff Up Your Library Media Center

3

Special Features in the Library Media Center

THE MILL HOUSE

Garrison Mill Elementary School
4111 Wesley Chapel Road
Marietta, GA 30062
Marie Madison, Library Media Specialist

Impetus for program.

The Garrison Mill Elementary School Library Media Center decided to celebrate reading and emphasize the school's theme by creating a mill house in the library media center. A notice was placed in *The Garrison Mill Gazette*, the school's newsletter, asking anyone interested in helping to build the mill house to contact the library media specialist. A father of two of the students volunteered to build the mill house using lumber donated by another father.

The "Mill House" at Garrison Mill Elementary School, Marietta, Georgia.

Implementation and description.

After preliminary construction elsewhere, the mill house was delivered to the school in eight pieces and assembled in the library media center. It was a small, roofed structure with half-high walls on three sides and a large mill wheel attached to the end wall. The opposite end was left open for a doorway. Inside, the mill house was furnished with a thick floor cushion, suitable for lying or sitting on. Several large throw pillows and stuffed animals provided comfortable surroundings for the students.

Inside the "Mill House" at Garrison Mill Elementary School, Marietta, Georgia.

Each teacher can give a special mill house pass to any student. The student then can go to the library media center for a period of time determined by the teacher to read silently inside the mill house.

Rules for using the mill house are simple:

— the student must possess a mill house pass

— the student must display good behavior in the library media center

— reading inside the mill house is to be done silently

Evaluation of program.

Students are eager to gain the special mill house passes. No matter what other activities are going on in the library media center, such as library media skills lessons or guest speakers, students using the mill house remain undisturbed. They seem to feel secluded and comfortable inside, continuing to read without interruption.

FIREPLACE AND SEATING IDEAS

Harbor Day School
3443 Pacific View Drive
Corona Del Mar, CA 92625
Anne Polkingharn, Library Director

Impetus for program.

The Harbor Day School library's primary emphasis is on books; therefore, it is thought of more as a library than as a media center. The library interior should provide an informal, home-like environment where students can relax and enjoy reading. They should be encouraged to regard the library as a pleasant place in which to spend their time. The architectural design and some of the interior furnishings were planned to accomplish this effect.

Implementation and description.

A "ski lodge" effect was created by the interior design, complete with a wood-burning fireplace in a comfortable, home-furnished reading and storytelling area.

The ski lodge effect and easily read signs (top); a wood-burning fireplace creates a homey atmosphere (bottom).

Large, easily read signs direct students to various parts of the 12,000-volume collection.

Emphasizing the library's orientation toward books and a comfortable reading atmosphere, large, cubical, foam pillows covered in soft, blue/gray woolen fabric with quilted tops are scattered in different areas. These cubes may be rearranged for sitting on or against, lying on, and putting together to suit the convenience of patrons of any size.

Students enjoying the informal atmosphere created by foam cubes. Harbor Day School, Corona Del Mar, California.

Evaluation of program.

The homelike design and informal foam cubes have been successful in attracting students to the library for their reading enjoyment.

THE LEPRECHAUN EXPRESS

Killearn Lakes Elementary School
8307 East Deerlake East
Tallahassee, FL 32312
Roberta Mann, Library Media Specialist

Impetus for program.

Our school desired to provide a child-oriented atmosphere in the library media center while encouraging the use of audiovisual materials. As we planned to have an Irish theme throughout the school, we selected a double-decker bus for the basic design of the proposed audiovisual center.

"Leprechaun Express" with space for 16 students to participate in various media activities. Killearn Elementary School, Tallahassee, Florida.

Implementation and description.

In discussions of purchases for the new library media center, our principal and the assistant media supervisor for the school district agreed to approve the outlay of some capital funds to construct the bus. This money would otherwise have been spent to purchase audiovisual carrels that matched the other furniture in the library media center.

The assistant media supervisor built a model of the bus from tagboard. This helped everyone understand exactly what it would look like and see the possibilities of its use. During the two years it took for the bus to become a reality, the model served to provide motivation for the staff and encouragement to everyone that we would someday have the bus in our library media center.

The draftsman from the company selected to build the bus studied a rough sketch and the model, as well as visiting nearby Oak Ridge Elementary School to see their audiovisual train, before he set to work. We were able to work consistently with him during the drafting period, clarifying ideas and details. Once the plans were drawn up, it took only a month to build the bus, which was transported to the school in sections.

The students had been shown the model and told that the bus was coming. Excitement ran high throughout the school. On the day the bus was assembled, a considerable number of students requested passes to the library media center to see it. Until the maintenance department was able to hook up the audiovisual connections for the bus, it was used as a quiet place to read and write. During this time, the student aides were trained to use all of the equipment that would be placed on the bus, so that later they could help the students as needed.

The principal was in charge of the official opening. She introduced special guests who had helped to make the bus possible and asked students for suggestions in naming it. When the library media center committee later sorted through the many good names submitted, three were voted on, and the Leprechaun Express became the official name.

The Express has eight compartments, each seating two students. The circulation desk supplies tickets that will admit two students at a time, after students have obtained a Media Bus pass from their teachers. Each compartment is set up for a different activity: two computers, two sound filmstrip projectors, one listening center, one "Speak and Spell," one "Speak and Math," and one "Speak and Read." Activities available are changed every two to four weeks.

Students using the "Leprechaun Express." Killearn Lakes Elementary School, Tallahassee, Florida.

Evaluation of program.

Students who finish their classroom work early may ask the teacher for a Media Bus pass, so the program has provided a considerable positive working impetus in the classroom. There are very few times during a school day when students are not on the bus. Occasionally, teachers have even been obliged to come and retrieve students who have stayed too long. The bus has provided easy access to audiovisual equipment and materials being used by a class for research projects.

In addition, the Leprechaun Express has become the focal point for many other activities. Class pictures have been taken in front of it, and it has also been used as a backdrop for locally produced video presentations.

Students have made audiovisual media use their top priority this year because of the presence of the bus, so next year we plan to place more emphasis on a balanced use of books and audiovisual materials in the library media center.

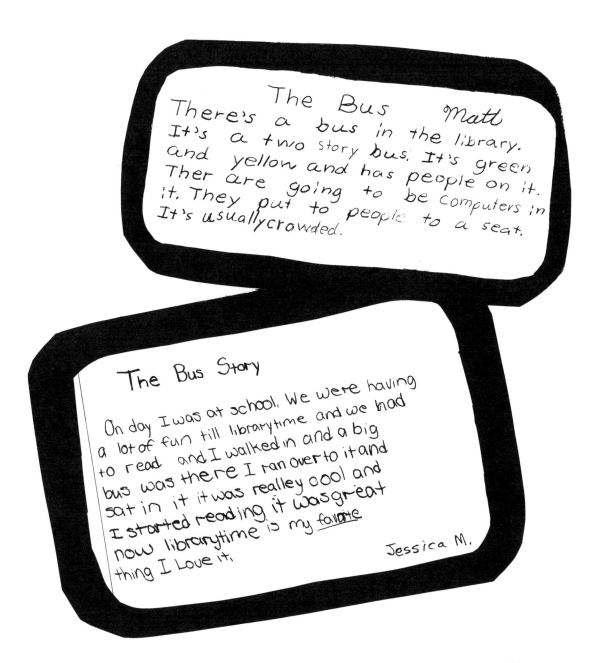

Student stories about the "Leprechaun Express." Killearn Lakes Elementary School, Tallahassee, Florida.

PAINTINGS AND SCULPTURES IN THE LIBRARY MEDIA CENTER

Miramar Ranch Elementary School
10770 Red Cedar Drive
San Diego, CA 92131
Carol Prock, Library Media Specialist

Impetus for program.

In 1976, a new school was planned for the Scripps Ranch area of San Diego. The library media center was designed as an integral part of the new Miramar Ranch Elementary School. The library media center has evolved gradually into the focal point of creative activities throughout the school. We planned to involve students and teachers in the creation of works of art to enhance the library media center. The projects included sculptures and replicas of famous paintings.

Implementation and description.

During the first three years the school was open, over one hundred students worked with teachers and aides to create "living pictures" by drawing and painting reproductions of famous works of art. These pictures, including replicas of paintings by Picasso, Gauguin, and Reni, grace our library media center.

Students from other classes have created striking life-sized papier-mâché sculptures of animals, including a giraffe, a kangaroo, and a unicorn. These sculptures were placed in the library media center, serving to welcome students as well as to indicate the location of their learning area for the day.

Kindergartners listening to "The Quilt Story" near the entrance where a student created papier-mâché kangaroo and unicorn are located, along with a student created painting of "The Young Bacchus." Miramar Ranch Elementary School, San Diego, California.

Recently, the library media center facilities were expanded to accommodate Apple and Commodore computers, a television studio with a closed-circuit television system for all classrooms, an audiovisual learning center, and an area focussing on library media skills activities.

Each morning, groups of about fifty students rotate through the several learning centers. Classes have assigned library media center time in the afternoons, during which students may return individually to take advantage of other resources. These include the extensive book collection, literary stories in video format, book talks given by the library media specialist, and oral stories told by the library media center staff each week.

A four-faced clock and ceiling hangings help create a homey atmosphere.

Evaluation of program.

The colorful and skillfully produced sculptures and paintings have added considerably to the atmosphere of the library media center. Students and teachers look forward to their scheduled visits to the center.

CABIN DAYS

Paul C. Garrison Elementary School
4138 Niewoehner Road
Richmond, IN 47374
Karen Montgomery, Library Media Specialist

Impetus for program.

In 1981, our school developed a special annual program to recreate the pioneer and native American life of the early 1800s in the Indiana area. The ambitious week-long educational treat was planned to include the whole school and was to be directed by the library media specialist in conjunction with the creative arts teacher, who helped to develop the program. The experience to be provided was multidisciplinary, requiring the cooperation of a host of resource people and the backing of the whole community to make it a success.

Implementation and description.

The school was able to acquire an authentic pioneer log cabin, built in 1806 by Quaker settlers John and Elvira Townsend, and move it onto the school grounds.

The cabin has become the focal point for the annual Cabin Days Celebration, held in October. Activities, demonstrations, and performances by volunteers from among area artists and crafters are scheduled throughout the week. Students are exposed to skills and understandings of pioneer and native American life, allowing them firsthand experience of what it was like to live in the Indiana of 175 years ago.

Local black powder enthusiasts come to demonstrate the operation of a flintlock muzzle-loader. Music and folk instruments traditional in the area are celebrated in several concerts, along with folk dancing.

Students have the opportunity to gain hands-on experience with common pioneer tools, such as using a drawknife to shave and shape wood. Whittling, carving, caning, and wood splitting are also demonstrated and taught.

Pioneer cooking, baking, apple-butter making, cider pressing, and the use of herbs are demonstrated, along with native American foods and cooking. Students may sample many of these foods as the dishes are prepared.

Recreation activities explore pioneer and native American games, the making of cornhusk dolls, and common recreation in home and school. The students may also participate in a Johnny Appleseed race and look-alike contest.

Industries and skills necessary to the survival of the pioneer family, who would have had little access to commercially produced goods, include quilt making, spinning, weaving, cloth dyeing, and candle making, as well as the careful planning and tending of a garden.

A Wyandot chief comes to address the students on various aspects of native American culture, and demonstrations of arrowhead making, basketry, and teepee erecting are included with lectures on archaeology and native American artifacts that have been found locally.

Other topics that may be demonstrated or provided as participatory events are outdoor drama, poetry reading, and storytelling.

Evaluation of program.

Through this educational celebration, the students receive a thrilling taste of pioneer life that makes local history and culture come alive in a way they will long remember.

In 1983, the program received the Esther V. Burrin Award of the Association of Indiana Media Educators for excellence in an Indiana school library media program. The program is readily adaptable to other schools, even those without access to a cabin or actual historic structure.

The Cabin Days Celebration at Paul C. Garrison Elementary School in Richmond, Indiana, featured a bluegrass concert; flintlock rifle demonstration; sampling of pioneer foods, such as venison; and a chance to use pioneer tools, such as a drawknife on a shaving horse.

THE TREE IN THE LIBRARY MEDIA CENTER

Woodville Elementary School
Woodville Road
Tallahassee, FL 32301
Wanda Phares, Library Media Specialist

Impetus for program.

The library media specialist wanted an outdoor theme and decided to create a life-sized tree to be placed inside the center. The tree was planned so that its construction and finishing would involve the students.

Students enjoying a large indoor tree. Woodville Elementary School, Tallahassee, Florida.

Implementation and description.

The basic structure of the tree was produced by welding aluminum conduit together. The welder then brought the tree into the library media center, where he spread out the limbs and roots with a pipe bender. This resulted in a free-standing tree that resembled a small wire tree sculpture.

Heavy-duty aluminum foil was wrapped about the conduit sculpture in large amounts to fill out the shapes of the tree trunk, large limbs, small limbs, and twigs. Cast padding obtained from a surgical supply house was wrapped about trunk and limbs over the aluminum foil and held in place by strong thread wrapped over it. When wrapped at various angles, the thread gave the appearance of tree bark.

The tree was then placed on sheets of plastic and sixteen quarts of extra-strength Elmer's glue were applied. This part of the operation turned out to be rather messy because the glue dripped from the limbs of the tree. In three weeks, the glue was dry and ready to be painted.

Students painted the tree with brown and black acrylic paint that was applied with sponges. They then made leaves from foil that was dark green on one side and light green on the other, attaching them to the tree by twisting green florist's wire around the ends of each leaf.

All of the materials that had to be purchased cost approximately $350, with the aluminum conduit and the welder's time being donated to the school.

Evaluation of program.

The tree provides a focal point for students' involvement in the library media center. They often provide items to put in the tree, such as nests, flowers, apples, and decorations for Christmas and Halloween. It has survived four years of children sitting on its roots and shows minimal damage. To increase durability of the roots, extra applications of glue or a clear acrylic are provided.

4

Special Themes in the Library Media Center

THE BERKELEY BEAR

Berkeley Lake Elementary School
4300 Berkeley Lake Road
Duluth, GA 30316
Joyce Kirkpatrick, Library Media Specialist

Impetus for program.

When our school opened in 1983, a bear was chosen as the school mascot. We decided to create a theme for the library media center using different sorts of bears.

Implementation and description.

It was simple to collect bears from here and there to decorate the sparsely filled shelves of our new library media center. Teachers were invited to bring their bears, each of which was given a name tag. Several parents also brought in bears, one an ancient, bedraggled bear more than seventy years old.

The bear theme caught the imagination of students and faculty of the school. At one point during the first year, several of the library media center bears were kidnapped and held for ransom by a faculty prankster, but the story had a happy ending and all of the bears were eventually returned safe and sound.

Even though the bears gave a warm atmosphere to the library media center, the walls remained uninteresting. As we could not afford to buy paintings with our small budget, we asked a volunteer parent artist to represent some famous literary bears on a wall panel. A 4' × 4' sheet of plywood was donated for the project, the library media center provided money for the paint, and the panel was brought in. We covered the finished product with a coat of polyurethane varnish and bolted it to the wall so that it could be moved when necessary.

Our yearly reading incentive program is entitled "Books Make Berkeley Bears Bright." Another parent volunteer created a banner of dancing pandas to emphasize this theme.

During Children's Book Week, we planned a special bear celebration. All of the students were invited to bring their bears in to spend the week in the library media center, and over 500 bears came to visit. Each was adorned with a special certificate, which the student was allowed to keep at the end of the week. We set up bear activity centers for the week's activities, including an estimation center where students guessed the number of gummy bears in a gallon jar. The classroom of the closest guesser received the whole jar of bears at the end of Children's Book Week.

For National Library Week, we scheduled a Celebrity Read-In. One celebrity was our school mascot, Berkeley Bear himself, who shared a book with the kindergarten class.

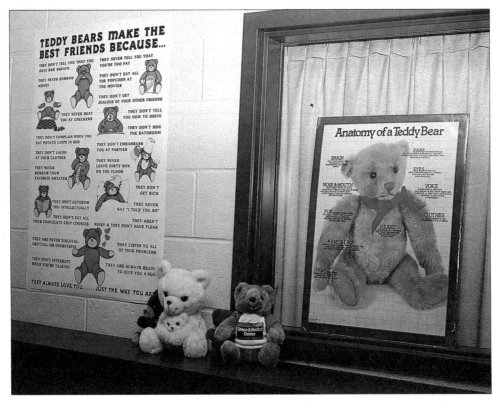

Bears of every size and description brighten the shelves and walls of the library media center. Berkeley Lake Elementary School, Duluth, Georgia.

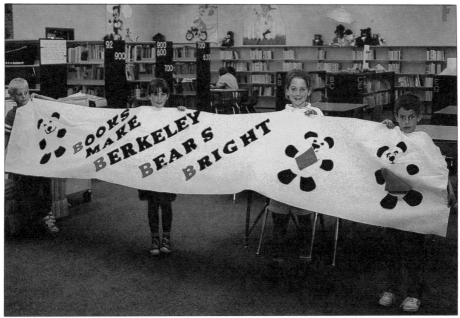

Dancing pandas banner created by a parent volunteer. Berkeley Lake Elementary School, Duluth, Georgia.

Evaluation of program.

The bears in the library media center have provided a focal point for themes and displays throughout the school year. Students, parents, and faculty have responded positively to their presence and have contributed new ideas for library media center use.

CREATING AN OPEN-SPACE LIBRARY MEDIA CENTER

Chehalem Elementary School
15555 S.W. Davis Road
Beaverton, OR 97005
Lorrie Holt, Library Media Specialist

Impetus for program.

Our library media center was physically too small for the school population, and its usefulness was further restricted by too much furniture and the poor use of interior space. It had been designed with no interior walls, to occupy an open space in the center of six open classroom areas.

Tables, chairs, bookshelves, and revolving paperback book racks cluttered the already cramped floor space, making it difficult for students to find books. Entire sections of the collection were not being checked out because of their inconvenient or obscure locations. As well, library media center administrative tasks and skills teaching were hampered by the lack of administrative space and the noise level from the six surrounding classrooms.

We planned a complete reorganization of existing space to correct these deficiencies. The project included removing the extra furniture, creating alternative seating arrangements, and allowing for different student use areas within the library media center. An administrative work area was created for the staff and the collection was made more accessible to students.

Implementation and description.

All but two of the table-and-chair sets were removed from the library media center. We bought enough bright denim fabric and polyester fiberfill for volunteers to make thirty large pillows and created a classroom/reading area with pillows. Extra pillows were piled up for students to arrange as they wished when curling up with a book. We provided oversized clipboards to use as hard writing surfaces.

Students enjoying one of several comfortable reading areas. Chehalem Elementary School, Beaverton, Oregon.

We moved most of the bookshelves in order to open up the interior floor space, making the fiction and general reading sections easier to locate and use, and the library media center's claustrophobic atmosphere was replaced by one of open space and room. The new arrangement allowed us to move the reference collection from its previous location, completely outside the center, to an L-shaped shelf section inside which the two remaining tables were placed. Here the students could come to do research and the quiet policy was strictly enforced.

Paperbacks were eventually moved to the tops of the low bookcases that formed the center's new interior walls, thus freeing more floor space as well as making the paperbacks easier to find and maintain.

In order to create more work space for library media center administration, we built a small, functional island that incorporated the three card catalogs, the kindergarten collection shelves, the desk, and the check-out tables. The interior provided space for administrative tasks, while the outside edges served the students. The placement of this island near the entrance created a quiet area in the rear corner that could then be used as a classroom for library media skills. We created at least an illusion of privacy and quiet for the classroom by facing the class away from the center entrance and backing the area with a sound-retarding panel and a papier-mâché sculpture.

Students who wish to work in small groups or share a book are encouraged to take a pillow and clipboard and settle on the floor near the fiction collection, which is now at the opposite end of the center from the classroom and quiet study areas.

Once the library media center was rearranged, it was easy to redecorate. Bright colors ring the perimeters and help to define special purpose areas. Large multicolored pictures created on butcher paper with the help of an opaque projector adorn the exterior walls, with plants and stuffed animals completing the decor.

Story time and video viewing area with colorful kites and stuffed animals. Chehalem Elementary School, Beaverton, Oregon.

Evaluation of program.

Our library media center program allows for a completely accessible center. Students know they may always come to the library media center, and further, it is a place they want to be.

The vital role of our library media center program is the fight against aliteracy: people who can read, but do not.

A MEDIEVAL THEME

Knight Elementary School
401 South River Road
Lilburn, GA 30247
Ruth Witmer, Library Media Specialist

Impetus for program.

Because our school name is Knight Elementary, we decided to use castles, knights, kings, and queens as the theme for our library media center. Our budget is always limited, so we planned to do most of the decorating with volunteer labor and inexpensive materials. Decorating with a theme would be time-consuming, but we would not be faced with the prospect of constantly pulling down and replacing extensive seasonal decorations. We decided to use the theme decorations to enhance the division of the library media center into different usable areas for the students.

Implementation and description.

Much of the decorating was done with cardboard, which we purchased in large sheets from a paper company. We bought white cardboard, which, although it cost slightly more than the brown variety, proved easier to spray-paint. We cut the cardboard to look like the walls of a castle and painted it with numerous cans of gray paint. Felt and stick-on letters made banners and flags. The cardboard walls had to be bolted into place to stabilize them.

Two huge felt banners with the letter "K" hang in the windows. A six-foot-tall cardboard herald greets students coming in the door and points to the Popcorn Proclamation, an incentive program for getting books returned on time. Each week that a class has no overdue books, it receives one letter in the word "popcorn." When the entire word is spelled, the class earns a movie and popcorn party.

An arch marks the entrance to the Easy Corner, where primary classes come for story time. A special round table enclosed by a wall made of plywood is designated by a banner, "Knights at the Round Table," and students may work on assignments in the castle enclosure. Cardboard fairy tale figures stand around the room.

File cabinets are enclosed in more castle wall cardboard, and a round tower made from an old flour barrel holds audiovisual materials as they are returned. Dragons perch over each window, a castle is represented on the back wall, and another herald announces the Royal Proclamation—the name and poster-sized picture of a student whose book recommendation is featured.

Posterboard flags over the nonfiction section are labeled with the names of the subjects below. Each class produces a shield, which we display in the center.

Evaluation of program.

A theme pulls the library media center together, and we occasionally add new items. We put up some seasonal decorations, but try to fit them into the theme. A theme also makes it easy for us to spot new ideas that can work for us. This year Rapunzel, with real braids, will go up over the entrance.

Examples of "Medieval theme" throughout the library media center. Knight Elementary School, Lilburn, Georgia.

USING COLOR AND TEXTURE TO IMPROVE ENVIRONMENT

Norton Elementary School
3050 Carson Road
Snellville, GA 30278
Faye S. Curlee, Library Media Specialist

Impetus for program.

Our school had a new library media center, with a small but growing book collection, that needed some decorative accents as well as features that would assist the students in using the collection.

Implementation and description.

To brighten the center and emphasize the location of the primary collection, we hung brightly colored balloon curtains from the ceiling, enclosing the easy section. Stuffed animal characters are displayed on shelves throughout the easy section to help students identify characters from the books.

The different subject areas of the nonfiction collection are highlighted by bright cloth banners on the ends of the bookshelves. These banners display the Dewey decimal numbers as well as pictures that indicate what the section contains.

Brightly colored banners with Dewey decimal numbers highlight ends of shelves.

Evaluation of program.

The bright decorations have enhanced the appearance of the library media center, making it more attractive to students. Learning aids located in the easy and nonfiction collections have proved invaluable in assisting the students to use these sections, and have also provoked their interest.

LIBRARY MEDIA CENTER ATMOSPHERE

Rock Chapel Elementary School
c/o DeKalb County School System
Decatur, GA 30032
Charlene K. Douglass, Library Media Specialist

Impetus for program.

Our library media center needed some decorative accents and seasonal theme decorations. We also planned features that would assist the students in using the collection.

Illustrated T-shirts, shadow boxes, and scroll stories are among the imaginative decorations. Rock Chapel Elementary School, Decatur, Georgia.

Implementation and description.

On the tops of shelves, especially in the nonfiction section, we have objects that students can look at and touch representing the contents of the books on those shelves. For example, over the 500s we put a terrarium, a bird's nest, sea shells, geodes, and fossils. We also display actual books from these categories. When students realize that these are hints about what is on the shelves they use the displays as markers, and many even volunteer to bring in things from their own collections to display and share.

On the wall beside the periodicals, we have a display of questions along with the location of the answers (name, date, and page of periodical). We try to make the questions interesting enough to motivate the students to look up the answers, changing the list monthly. This makes an attractive display that complements the periodicals, as well as fostering research skills. A sample question would be "How long ago was the world's oldest ship sealed in a tomb in Egypt?" Students are directed to the *National Geographic*, April 1988, pp. 529-533 for the answer.

The U.S. Postal Service, IBM, and RIF (Reading Is Fundamental) sponsored the Summer of the Readasaurus, which included a traveling dinosaur egg and prizes for summer reading. As a tie-in to this theme, we made a huge papier-mâché egg and put it in a large nest in a chickenwire cage, which was placed on the circulation desk with a note that mentioned the hatching date. The poster "READ: AVOID EXTINCTION" and the Summer of the Readasaurus information were nearby. Students of all ages checked the egg daily for signs of hatching, trying to guess what would come out. At the end of the week, a Readasaurus (a 15"-high dinosaur made of felt) came out of the egg with a small book it was reading. We involved the students in a contest to name the Readasaurus, giving books as prizes.

A good springtime display we have used includes a colorful windsock hung from the ceiling with a variety of book covers attached to its streamers. A 50'-long cellophane kite wraps around two walls, with the theme banner "Fly High with Books" displayed below.

A glass display case is perfect for showing off old and delicate books to attract students' interest. The books are propped up to show the covers or the stories inside, with small cards telling students when and where the books were published and some important historical events that happened in the year of publication. The books are treated as though they are on closed reserve, and students are therefore able to look at the books in the center.

Evaluation of program.

The decorations and various displays attract the attention of students and encourage them to get involved with the library media center collection. Their desire to read is stimulated by the programs and displays, in which they are able to participate actively.

5

Learning Centers in the Library Media Center

LEARNING CENTERS AND STUDENT INVOLVEMENT

Gwin Oaks Elementary School
400 Gwin Oaks Drive
Lawrenceville, GA 30245
Nancy Wayte, Library Media Specialist

Impetus for program.

The philosophy at Gwin Oaks is that the library media center should be an "enrichment center." The library media specialist works cooperatively with the teachers to produce relevant centers that are planned around themes related to classroom curricula, library media skills, literature appreciation, special days and celebrations, recreation and games, music and art, and computers. Facilities were planned to allow for twenty-five centers to operate at one time. The number available at any given time varies, depending upon the time required to set them up and the space needed for other school activities. All centers are adapted or changed monthly.

Implementation and description.

The students are allowed time out of the classroom to investigate centers that interest them or that are assigned by the teacher. They are given a pass stating the purpose of their visit, the time allowed, and the specific centers they should complete.

The "Book Tub" is a fun reading place. Gwin Oaks Elementary School, Lawrenceville, Georgia.

A science center may include live animals and fish and affords opportunities for looking up information about the animals, sharing pictures of students' pets, and creative writing about animals, as well as bringing in students' own pets.

Another center emphasizes particular authors, different types of literature, and characters from books, while an art center has crayons available for drawing pictures related to literature. Games teaching library media skills are available from the games shelf.

The children's literature center displays names and addresses of authors of children's books so that students can write to the authors. Replies are displayed on a bulletin board and later organized into a scrapbook.

Audiovisual equipment is set up for use at all times and the students are trained to use it as soon as possible, making constant staff supervision unnecessary.

Notes and posters are used to entice students toward special centers or activities. These are placed around the school as well as in the library media center, inviting the students to visit a center, share something with others, try some research, or be ready for a special occasion.

Learning centers for library media skills attract student interest. Gwin Oaks Elementary School, Lawrenceville, Georgia.

Evaluation of program.

Students, teachers, and paraprofessionals who use the program provide constant feedback as to its effectiveness. Many teachers and aides use the centers with students on a weekly basis, specifically planning for their incorporation into the curriculum. The library media center is child-oriented, taking into account the uniqueness of each student. Students are encouraged to pursue interests that will involve them in a quest for lifelong learning.

INTEGRATING LIBRARY
MEDIA SKILLS

Willow Woods Elementary School
11001 Daniel Drive
Sterling Heights, MI 48077
Jeanette Mateer, Library Media Specialist

Impetus for program.

District philosophy advocates flexible scheduling and a curriculum guide provides broad guidelines for planning activities to be offered at each level. Much of the library media program is planned to integrate skills with literature promotion.

Implementation and description.

Small group scheduling is planned to dovetail with teacher reading groups. For example, both first grades send their low reading groups on Mondays, middle reading groups on Tuesdays, and high reading groups on Wednesdays. Whole classes are scheduled in for unit introductions for special subject teaching programs.

Our four huge bulletin boards are used as participation projects whenever possible. One board is set aside for constantly changing "challenges." For several years we enlarged the monthly calendar from *Instructor* for this board, expanding on the questions for each day. The first student to research the question and turn in the correct answer had his or her name displayed on the board and earned a sticker. "Problem Parade," from Dale Seymour, is providing mental stimulation this year. We provide teachers with the warm-up and follow-up activities for class use.

Participation bulletin board based on monthly calendar from *Instructor*. Willow Woods Elementary School, Sterling Heights, Michigan.

Most library media instruction units change from year to year. A Winter Olympics unit, which is research-oriented, is offered every four years, as is a Paddington unit. The Caldecott unit for third graders and the Mother Goose unit for the first grade are so popular that we usually do them annually, with some variation.

The dragon was constructed by the high school students for a Medieval Feast and donated to our school in time for our "Dragons, Dinosaurs, and Mysterious Monster" Unit. Willow Woods Elementary School, Sterling Heights, Michigan.

The Caldecott unit challenges the students to read or have read to them all of the winning titles. They learn to write a summary for each story read and the summaries are used to track progress. Many stories are shared through audiovisual media or read aloud by teachers or the library media specialist. We frequently extend the stories through art or writing activities. At the unit culminating party, we share the most recent Caldecott, decorate "Wild Things" cookies, and have a Caldecott Challenge, using electronic buzzer boards in a game that asks content questions taken from the Caldecott books.

Library media center skills are integrated into the program as much as possible. We introduce the total collection and card catalog to the third grade, beginning with two library media center awareness activities. Each reading group is then scheduled in for eight consecutive days of hands-on card catalog instruction.

Evaluation of program.

Not all faculty members are as enthusiastic about the library media integration program as is the third grade, so intensity of use varies at other levels.

We are still in the process of achieving the goal of the library media program: to be a true extension of the classroom curriculum.

6

Reading Incentive Activities in the Library Media Center

DEWEY FASHIONATA

Austin Elementary School
5435 Roberts Drive
Dunwoody, GA 30338
Barbara Kaden, Library Media Specialist

Impetus for program.

Our library media center was in need of new ideas to teach as a part of our flexibly scheduled library media skills program. One of the library media specialists suggested letting the students make T-shirts and we began to look for ways to put this idea into practice. When a local department store's advertisement for a fashion show called "Rich's Fashionata" came to our attention, we decided to adapt the idea as a fashion show for T-shirts related to library media skills.

Implementation and description.

The first year we planned to hold the Dewey Fashionata, the sixth and seventh grades were scheduled regularly for library media classes, so we decided to limit the program to those levels.

Upon completion of a library media skills unit emphasizing the Dewey decimal classification system, students were assigned a block of Dewey numbers (e.g., 700s), or the fiction/easy categories. We found that the assigned numbers had to be recorded and monitored to prevent students from swapping numbers indiscriminately, producing, for example, an inordinately large number of young male students making T-shirts in the 700s.

A handout gave the necessary information: a synopsis of the planned Fashionata, materials and costs, project due date, and suggestions on where to purchase T-shirts and paints. We provided at least one month to work on the T-shirts to allow for unexpected obstacles.

The next time the class met students were to select any book in the category they were assigned. Each book selected was then placed on the reserve shelf for future use. Students would find a reproducible picture, preferably a line drawing, and use an overhead or opaque projector to project the image so it could be drawn onto a T-shirt. Original art work was also permitted. Students could use crayons, sometimes ironing the design from the inside to produce unusual effects; washable acrylic paints; magic markers; puff paints; and various 3-D objects such as flannel and sequins to create their chosen designs.

We arranged with the art teacher to allow time for completion of the T-shirts, since the library media skills classes met only once a week. When completed, T-shirts were stored in the art room, with students' names attached.

Student using the opaque projector to enlarge illustration to be painted on T-shirt.

Art teacher working with students in the creation of "Dewey Fashionata" T-shirts. Austin Elementary School, Dunwoody, Georgia.

The Dewey Fashionata was an actual fashion show in which students walked across the stage showing off their T-shirt masterpieces to a panel of judges. We played popular songs as a background during the show.

The kindergarten students assisted with the introduction of the program. A student or a small group of children walked across the stage with items depicting each category while a commentator identified the category, which would also be shown on the back of each student's T-shirt.

The entire school, including parents and other community members, was invited to watch the fashion show. Faculty from nearby schools were invited well in advance to judge the show. We had two tables of three judges, each with a student runner. One panel would watch a category of T-shirts, while the other panel completed their remarks on the previous category. Judges considered originality, appropriateness of design to category, and overall appearance.

We served refreshments to the judges in the library media center, thus helping with public relations. Students were awarded prizes donated by local merchants and the PTA.

Evaluation of program.

Students, parents, and teachers displayed a great deal of enthusiasm, requesting that the Dewey Fashionata become an annual event. Test scores in library skills increased throughout the school.

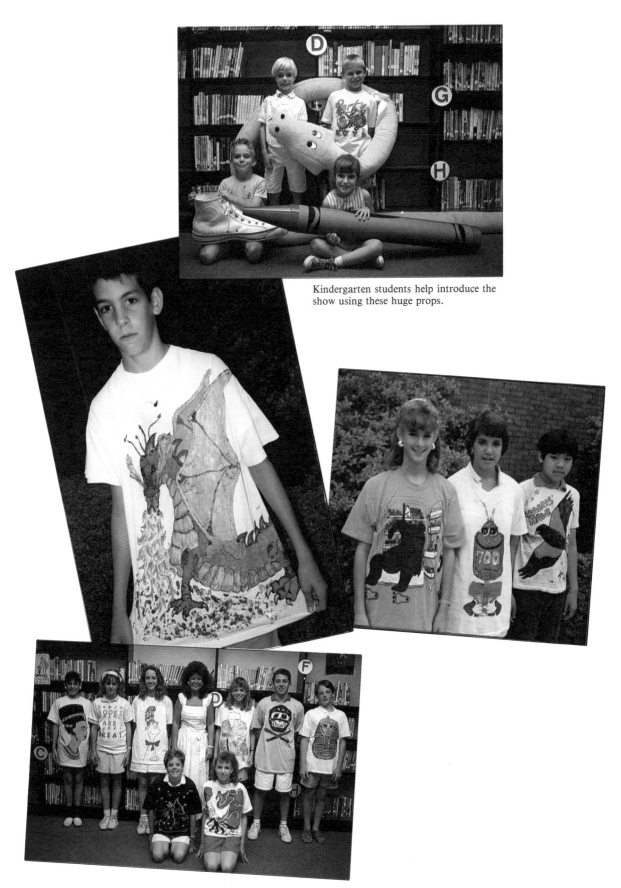

Kindergarten students help introduce the show using these huge props.

A wide variety of creations adorned T-shirts at the "Dewey Fashionata." Austin Elementary School, Dunwoody, Georgia.

Program used when parents came for the presentation of the "Dewey Fashionata." Austin Elementary School, Dunwoody, Georgia.

BATTLE OF BOOKS

Cumberland Elementary School
700 East Golf Road
Des Plaines, IL 60016
Bridget Doerner, Library Media Specialist

Impetus for program.

Plans for the Battle of Books began in 1977. We collected information from Urbana and Elgin public libraries on their programs and redesigned them for our use. We also invited two libraries from Winnetka to tell us about their programs.

Implementation and description.

As a team, the library media specialists interested in the program selected forty titles to use. These were checked for paperback availability so that several copies could be purchased for each building. The library media specialists divided the titles among themselves and wrote approximately twenty-five questions from each title, using the "In what book ..." format.

We begin our program in November during Children's Book Week, with questions from ten of the forty books. In January, we have battles with questions from another ten books. We do the third set of ten in February and the last set in March.

Our teams consist of three students from the fourth, fifth, and sixth grades. Any group of three may make themselves into a team and challenge any other team. When we get a winning team from each classroom, we hold school tournaments to determine first-, second-, and third-place winners. The public library holds a reception for all of the winning teams in the district, inviting a local author to speak.

The games consist of twenty questions, ten for each team. The team is given fifteen seconds to answer. If they cannot, the question is saved in case of a later tie. Five points are given for the correct title and three points for the author.

Keeping score during the Battle of Books. Cumberland Elementary School, Des Plaines, Illinois.

Winning teams are presented with certificates and the participants' names are publicized throughout the school. The first-place team's name is engraved on a wall plaque.

Evaluation of program.

The games progress very quickly and are very exciting. We have found that we need to be well prepared in order to conduct them properly.

Non-readers are as interested in watching the battles as are avid readers. Many come to the library media center when the battles are over, asking to check out the books that were used. The Battle of Books is an effective method of interesting children in reading.

LIBRARY EXPEDITION
AND CAMP-IN

Hunter Elementary School
1630 Gillam Way
Fairbanks, AK 99701
Barbara L. Gorman, Library Media Specialist

Impetus for program.

The basic idea for the program originated when the library media specialist was looking for a suitable activity to celebrate National Library Week. A similar program involving student camp-ins at a museum had been used in Boston and could be adapted to our local public library, Noel Wein Public Library, in Fairbanks.

Implementation and description.

We obtained the approval of the principal and the school district, then approached the public library director, the mayor, and local legal counsel. Following legal advice, we drew up parent permission forms for student participation.

Included in staffing for the project were the school principal, the children's librarian of the public library, our school's reading resource teacher, one sixth-grade teacher, and one parent volunteer. Six students from the children's literature class at the University of Alaska volunteered to act as group leaders and chaperones.

The basic goal was to increase our sixth-grade students' awareness of the importance of libraries. We would provide the students with a unique "inside-out" view of the public library, offer information on the various collections within it, and familiarize them with appropriate tools available for library use.

At 6:30 on a Friday evening, the students arrived at the public library to check in and select their breakfast for the next morning. This was followed by a group tour of the library and then the participants were divided into three small study groups.

From 7:30 to 9:00, the groups attended three thirty-minute workshops on catalog use, story-telling, and library acquisitions and special collections. At 9:15 the groups competed in a trivia contest designed to test their knowledge from the library tour and workshops. Refreshments were served at 9:45; at 10:15 there was a film presentation.

Participants were assigned to sleeping areas at 11:00 and lights out was at 11:30, but reading under the covers with a flashlight was definitely encouraged. The next morning, the students were awakened at 6:30 and served breakfast, which was donated by one of the local fast-food franchises.

Students were provided the opportunity to check out books they had found the night before and then were picked up by their parents at 8:00 a.m.

Evaluation of program.

The event received very favorable coverage from local news media and the staff of the public library indicated that they will happily endorse a second annual camp-in. Campers and parents called the camp-in an unqualified success, and we plan to make it an annual event.

Campers from Hunter Elementary School, Fairbanks, Alaska, preparing for the "Camp-In." Noel Wein Public Library, Fairbanks.

READING INCENTIVE PROJECT

Kennesaw Elementary School
6997 Keene Street
Kennesaw, GA 30144
Guelda McConnell, Library Media Specialist

Impetus for program.

As the library media center is a focal point of the school, the principal suggested having a replica of the school's mascot built as a quiet reading center. Our mascot is the Civil War locomotive "The General." The original locomotive, famous for the daring theft of her cargo by the Andrews Raiders during the Civil War, is located in the Big Shanty Museum in Kennesaw.

"The General" under construction by North Cobb High School industrial arts students. Kennesaw Elementary School, Kennesaw, Georgia.

Implementation and description.

The local high school industrial arts teacher was asked to let his students make the replica of the engine. They used a sketch drawn up by a PTA volunteer to draw plans, and parents were asked to donate lumber, nails, and paint. The high school also donated some materials. Photographs of the original locomotive were used to copy the details and color scheme.

The replica is nine feet long, six feet tall, and four and a half feet wide. We made cushions for students to sit on in the cab. Black 3" × 5" planks were made to look like railroad ties and brace the base of the engine.

The library media specialist and teachers decided to use the engine as a reward for good work in the classroom. We made tickets and distributed them to all teachers, who then determine when a student can come to read in The General.

Evaluation of program.

The program has been highly successful. Students enjoy coming to read in the cab of the locomotive, and it has served as a focal point for all visitors coming into the school.

READ-A-SAURUS
INCENTIVE PROGRAM

Ocoee Elementary School
400 South Lakewood Street
Ocoee, FL 32761
Cindy B. Booz, Library Media Specialist

Impetus for program.

The library media program consultant suggested we develop a new reading incentive program to replace the county program we had been using. Most children enjoy studying dinosaurs, the dinosaur section of the library media center was well stocked, and many new dinosaur products were hitting the market. Our principal also demonstrated interest in using a dinosaur theme. When the school district and the public library decided to develop a program to encourage young children to obtain library cards, we made plans to use the dinosaur theme for it.

Implementation and description.

To determine how many students already had public library cards, each classroom teacher took a tally during the first week. We discovered that 188 students out of 565 already had cards.

A kindergarten teacher and her daughter made a life-sized replica of a young Tyrannosaurus Rex from butcher paper and paint. After winter vacation, the children came back to find this huge creature greeting them in the library media center. Its purpose was explained by the principal during our morning announcements program.

Replica of a young Tyrannosaurus Rex. Ocoee Elementary School, Ocoee, Florida.

To emphasize the program to first graders, the library media specialist used dinosaur books and activities. We shared *Jethro's Difficult Dinosaur*, by Arnold Sundgaard; *Danny and the Dinosaur*, by Syd Hoff; *If Dinosaurs Were Cats and Dogs*, by Colin McNaughton; and *The Tyrannosaurus Game*, by Steven Kroll. Skills taught included alphabetizing the names of dinosaurs and learning the nonfiction location of dinosaur books, information on a title page, and the difference between fiction and nonfiction books.

Learning centers were set up in the library media center to help students of all ages learn more about dinosaurs. We used filmstrips, a dinosaur floor puzzle, dinosaur flash cards, a separate display of dinosaur books, and a dinosaur diorama at the circulation desk.

Each grade level was assigned a large section of bulletin board in the library media center to create a bulletin board display that encouraged reading. One class displayed a baby dinosaur being pushed in a carriage by its mother, with the caption "Get 'Em While They're Young." The curriculum resource clerk and her daughter made the main bulletin board, which carried the caption "Don't Let Your Mind Become Extinct ... Be a Read-a-Saurus."

At the end of the month we took another tally to find that twenty-nine additional students had obtained library cards, and many students had gained a greater awareness of the public library and its services.

Evaluation of program.

When we do the program again, we would like to plan field trips to the public library and invite the children's librarian from the branch library to talk with the children or do stories with them. We would also like to expand the program so that it would be more of a reading incentive program rather than merely a program to promote obtaining a library card. This would require more communication with parents, since they will have to drive their children to the public library for cards and books.

Media specialist and media clerk with first graders and their display. Ocoee Elementary School, Ocoee, Florida.

7

Integrating the Library Media Program into the Curriculum

INTEGRATING CURRICULUM UNITS

Blanche E. Fuqua Elementary School
1111 Wheeler Avenue
Terre Haute, IN 47802
Judith Ann Summers, Library Media Specialist

Impetus for program.

We designed a program to accomplish three goals to complement our instructional program. We wished to provide a system of flexible scheduling, to allow children to get materials for instructional and recreational needs; to increase motivation of children to read and appreciate various forms of literature; and to strengthen continuity of skills.

Implementation and description.

Every program is considered first by the school library media committee, recommended by the library media specialist, and approved by the principal. Committee members are highly supportive of the library media program, and they, rather than the library media specialist, present ideas to the faculty.

Each class is scheduled into the library media center for one hour a day on five consecutive days during the semester, providing continuity in lessons and skills. Special area teachers (art, music, etc.) were consulted so that the schedules do not conflict.

The units were coordinated with the classroom teacher. During the unit, teachers, classroom aides, and the library media specialist work as a team to accomplish the unit's goal.

The library media specialist confers with the grade level teachers to plan a unit. For example, at the third-grade level a local history unit is offered on Bill Peet, a local author. Children read his books, try recipes related to the time about which he wrote, make puppets and other art of characters in the books, and look up other material about him in the library media center. Teachers, students, and the library media specialist gather materials to do each unit.

The unit is taught by the library media specialist, with the teacher helping students during an activity such as making puppets or cookies. Lesson plans are recorded on a word processor so they can be modified as necessary each time the unit is taught.

Second graders are looking at the finished Ezra Jack Keats's book which they made using the collage method as Keats did for *The Snowy Day*. Blanche E. Fuqua Elementary School, Terre Haute, Indiana.

Evaluation of program.

Measurement procedures vary, but the most concrete is counting circulation of books after the unit is complete, not only during the remainder of the present year but also during the following year to assess carry-over interest.

Some former students have related that they have kept their projects through the years. Ideas and folders are often used for a college class. Teachers have been unanimously in favor of keeping and expanding the program. Parents have demonstrated increased interest and participation in the library media center.

INTEGRATION OF MEDIA INTO THE CURRICULUM

Oak Grove Elementary School
1301 West 104th Street
Bloomington, MN 55431
Thea Holtan, Library Media Specialist

Impetus for program.

By 1970, each elementary school in the Bloomington School District had a full-time library media specialist with four hours of daily clerical help. The newly developed audiovisual equipment attracted a lot of attention. Resource centers were developed and aimed at teaching students and teachers how to operate equipment, how to view and hear materials, and how to select good media. The goal was to cause an interaction between students and media so that students would know where and how to locate information.

Open access is crucial for the efficiency of a program. These fourth grade students use the nylon-pocket display of computer disks to find the disk which they need. Their teacher has sent them into the Skill-Development Lab to strengthen a math skill which they have been learning in class. All students use this open system, beginning in kindergarten, to enhance their self-reliance and develop self-esteem. Oak Grove Elementary School, Bloomington, Minnesota.

Implementation and description.

Oak Grove Elementary began to develop its library media center in 1974. The instructional role of the center had three facets: to teach by transfer of curricular skills and knowledge, to use skills that deliberately foster self-reliance, and to cause students to enhance and extend their learning styles.

Over the next six years we accomplished several basics in pursuit of these goals. Equipment was set up in a systematic and efficient way to provide easy use. Five areas were arranged and identified with 4'×4' signs hanging from the ceiling: Reading, Listening and Viewing, Small Groups, Reference, and Production.

We designed kits for students to use in learning reference and study skills, using a specific research process to gather information, interpret it, arrange it, and write reports using it.

Planning for the year began during pre-school workshop week, meeting teachers' instructional needs. More clerical time was contributed through the PTA, supplying another person for the library media center.

A skills development lab was designed for independent study use, and a media production area was developed for student productions in 35mm, video, audio, and photography.

The next three years saw growth and improvement. By the ninth year of operation, we had a fully developed library media center program. Computers and videocassettes began to be a part of teaching and we designed more activities. Finally, during the last five years, advances in technology have improved our image and made us indispensable.

Staff were given critiques of all the student computer programs. Books were barcoded for automated circulation. Thirty computers were put into the skills development lab and all of the lab's activities were computerized for location by skill and learner characteristics. Reading objectives were computerized for testing and monitoring.

We designed first-grade research with slides as the information source, causing students to examine criteria, substantiate observations, and orally present knowledge to classmates. Students' research reports, beginning in second grade, began to incorporate steps of self-examination for errors.

Evaluation of program.

The next few years should bring to reality a dream we have had for several years. Teachers apply for funds from contingency budgets and the school is awarded money to pay for release time so that the staff can work together throughout the year. We will design activities to replace worksheets, causing students to go to the library media center to practice, apply, transfer, and use reading skills while learning them. The current program is very exciting, but these plans are intended to give it a very practical dimension, truly integrated with the curriculum.

LIBRARY MEDIA CENTER INVOLVEMENT
IN HOLISTIC EDUCATION

Robbins Elementary School
Cummings Street
Robbins, NC 27325
Joyce Harris, Library Media Specialist

Impetus for program.

The state of North Carolina is concerned that students receive a holistic education. Integrating instruction throughout the whole school is a major focus. Our classroom teachers inform the library media specialist, art teacher, and other support teachers as to what is currently being studied and those topics are integrated with library media skills, art, and other special classes.

Implementation and description.

The county held workshops prior to school opening to inform teachers about integrating instruction in their classrooms. Our school faculty then discussed how we would implement our program. We finally decided that asking teachers periodically for their study topics seemed to work best.

Library media instruction is scheduled for each class for thirty minutes a week. Literature and media skills are planned to enrich and extend the units being studied in the regular classroom.

We have implemented a special project in the afternoons three days a week for two weeks so that the library media specialist can work with a select group of students all from the same grade level. After two months another group is chosen from a different grade level. Examples of topics studied in this special project are tigers for the third grade and study skills for the second grade. One of the goals is to produce a project to share with the rest of the school.

The art teacher contributes the children's art projects, which have been integrated with units studied in the library media center and the regular classroom. The art projects are displayed in the center.

The only change made to the library media center for the program was a clothesline erected between the rows of study carrels. Eight-foot metal poles were attached to the backs of three carrels, with a clothesline running from pole to pole. This has created a focal point, in addition to existing bulletin boards, for banners, children's art work, and posters.

Clothesline and poles which have created a focal point for study carrels. Robbins Elementary School, Robbins, North Carolina.

Evaluation of program.

Informal surveys of teachers and the principal are the only evaluations completed at this time. Those who commented were positive. The children involved in the special projects were eager to come to the library media center, some of them improving and completing their class work in order to be allowed to come.

8

Television Activities in the Library Media Center

THE "GOOD MORNING LEMIRA" SHOW

Lemira Elementary School
Fulton Street
Sumter, SC 29150
Randa Edmonds, Library Media Specialist

Impetus for program.

A few years ago, Lemira Elementary School was known as the little school down on Boulevard Road. Some people in the district didn't even know how to find the school. Located in the lowest socio-economic area of Sumter, we were expected to remain last in test scores and student attendance. Generally, however, faculty and staff morale remained high. Excellent classroom instruction was in evidence, but something was still missing.

Through the years, the PTO had purchased a color television set for each classroom for instructional use. It became apparent that with the addition of a color video camera the school could have its own television station. A live broadcast every morning would enable the school of 800 students and faculty to have an assembly and faculty meeting at the beginning of each day without leaving the classroom. This would allow the principal to immediately address problems as they arose and to praise students and faculty for accomplishments.

Implementation and description.

The "Good Morning Lemira" ("GML") show began in 1985 in a small workroom in the library. The first few shows were more of a news-anchor type reporting of school events by the principal. Seeing the principal in a friendly manner every morning helped to promote positive student-teacher-principal relationships.

We spread word that a puppet was needed to act as a student to converse with the principal. Many puppets were sent in to try out for the show, the one that captured the students' attention being a hand puppet that resembled a monkey.

A contest was held to name the monkey and the winning name was Banana Bob, submitted by a third-grade class. Banana Bob immediately became a daily co-host and student advocate. Later a puppet of the school mascot, a lion, was added to rotate with Banana Bob. The momentum of the show gradually grew and students, faculty, and other guests, such as the mayor, were featured on the show.

Eventually special weekly segments were added. One was the Lemira Derby, featured every Monday, which is an attendance race. Each class is represented by a horse on a chart. When a class has perfect attendance for one week, the horse is moved up a space. The first class to reach the finish line wins a pizza party, compliments of Pizza Hut.

The Wednesday feature is the Student of the Week. Each classroom teacher chooses one student who meets certain requirements. As the students are introduced on the show, their pictures are taken by a black-and-white video printer.

A third segment is Math Whiz. This was designed as a schoolwide activity to provide students with an incentive to develop speed and accuracy in computation. Every Friday students in grades one through five are given timed tests at the end of the "GML" show. These weekly tests are used as guided instructional tools for both teachers and students to assess accomplishment of objectives.

The Creative Thinking Skills segment is also very popular. One of the district coordinators appears on the show periodically. He challenges the students to give unusual responses to a phrase such as "things that can be split." His prop for that day might be a banana split. The classes have a given number of seconds to think and a given number of minutes to respond. The class with the most unusual answers wins.

"GML" begins promptly at 8:10, five minutes before school officially starts. All programs have an introduction that consists of scenes videotaped in the Sumter area set to the theme by John Williams that is used for "NBC Nightly News." The daily information consists of school events, student announcements, faculty announcements, birthdays, the day in history, and the lunch menu. The special daily and weekly segments are featured along with the music video. At the conclusion of the show, the P.E. teacher hosts PERK, which stands for Physical Exercise Revives Kids. This is a prerecorded segment to which the entire school exercises for five minutes.

All shows are recorded for the pre-school and kindergarten students, who only come to school for half a day. They are played back at 9:00 and again at 12:00.

Students are used in all positions except as host. A fourth grader operates the camera and two fifth graders work in the control room.

The field coordinator for ITV and a library media specialist ran appropriate cables and determined the correct hookups.

The color scheme reflects the school colors, which are royal blue and white. The stage curtain is a deep blue. The sunrise is painted bright orange and yellow, with white clouds.

Background set for morning television show. Lemira Elementary School, Sumter, South Carolina.

Evaluation of program.

There are many positive aspects to a daily live television show. Tardiness has decreased and attendance has increased. Daily student attendance was 95.2 percent in 1984 and has risen to more than 97 percent since the implementation of the "GML" show and the Lemira Derby.

The whole concept of the television show practically eliminates notes in teacher mailboxes, offering a quick and easy way to communicate with the whole school. It also promotes school pride, the principal is placed in a positive light, and student achievement is recognized. All students know what is happening in their school. Visitors to the school are featured on the program so everyone can recognize them.

We are constantly striving to improve the show. Television is a wonderfully flexible medium that can be tailored to each individual school's needs and preferences. The only limit is one's imagination. We have had many visitors come to Lemira to observe the show and study the set-up; several have returned to their schools to begin their own shows. In the future, we would like to develop a statewide Elementary Network News and network our shows with other schools.

VIDEO PRODUCTIONS IN THE LIBRARY MEDIA CENTER

Mayport Junior High School
2600 Mayport Road
Atlantic Beach, FL 32233
Janet Rowland, Library Media Specialist

"Welcome to Our School" Video Program

Impetus for program.

Mayport Junior High serves a unique population that includes 50 percent military dependents and consequently has approximately a 57 percent student-body turnover during the school year. We felt that transferring students should be assisted in achieving a smooth transition into the life of our school throughout the school year.

Implementation and description.

In order to achieve our goal, the library media center developed a welcome program that includes a student-produced video introducing key administrators and taking students on a tour of the school.

Evaluation of program.

The program has been evaluated through interviews and questionnaires given to students and parents. Very positive responses have been received. Our principal has received many suggestions about programs in schools from which new students have transferred and has enjoyed sharing the video and welcome bags with principals from other schools. Each year the new student council president revises the video with the assistance of the crew of the school video class.

Electronic Encyclopedia Activities

Impetus for program.

For several years students in the seventh- and eighth-grade compensatory education program have had a library media center assignment in biographical research. Students were required to use several sources, including traditional reference materials, periodicals, and the general collection. In order to assist and encourage productivity and greater success, we believed that introducing students to an electronic database, specifically the Grolier Academic American Encyclopedia (Electronic Encyclopedia), would spark enthusiasm.

Implementation and description.

In order to obtain the Electronic Encyclopedia, we applied for a grant, which was approved.

Working closely with the compensatory education teacher, we planned time in the library media center for the students in her five classes for two weeks.

One of the most important aids for students was the cross-referencing and listing of articles containing information about the people they were researching. The quick response time and accuracy of information were also benefits.

The cost of the Electronic Encyclopedia is approximately $1,000, including the cost of the Phillips CD-ROM player. It can be updated yearly for a nominal fee.

Evaluation of program.

The evaluation of the project was done by comparing the research papers of students who used the Electronic Encyclopedia with the papers of those who did not. This comparison considered the percentage of students who completed the assignment; bibliographies (number and variety); materials gathered; grades; and interviews with the students to assess their reactions to computer access to encyclopedia information.

Students found the database's requirement for correct spelling to be a disadvantage. Also, information was not available on several subjects.

Student using an electronic encyclopedia. Mayport Junior High School, Atlantic Beach, Florida.

Reading Incentive Program

Impetus for program.

Each year students in the seventh grade participate in the Florida Sunshine State Award Book Program. From a list of twenty books nominated by library media specialists across the state, students must read at least three titles to participate in voting for the award-winning book. To encourage students to read and participate in the voting, we thought a special computer voting booth might be an added incentive.

Implementation and description.

We asked a seventh-grade student who had been very involved in our after-school computer program all year to develop a voting program for the Sunshine State Books. We advertised the fact that voting would be by computer and used the Sunshine State logo and blue-and-yellow color scheme along with colored book-cover replicas on the library media center display.

Evaluation of program.

The students were intrigued with the method of voting, which automatically recorded the book with the highest number of votes each period. Our computer whiz was properly recognized by his fellow students for his contribution to the reading program, and we will certainly use the program again next year.

Video News and Annual

Impetus for program.

In the spring of 1988, Mayport Junior High produced a video annual for the first time. This was a natural outcome of the year-long taping of school events by students in the video journalism class.

Implementation and description.

The main product of the class is their fifteen-minute program "News and Views," which is networked from the library media center office to English classes once a month. Highlights of these programs were included in the video annual.

In its first year the video class earned first-place honors at the county media districtwide competition and went on to place second in the video category (junior high) when the Jim Harbin Awards were presented at the 15th Annual Conference of Florida School Media Specialists in 1987. Their entry in the contest was one of the "News and Views" programs.

Evaluation of program.

Students in the class learn all aspects of video production, including storyboard writing and scripting, directing, interviewing, editing, and special effects. The PTA co-sponsors the video annual, providing the blank tapes for duplicating.

SPOOK HILL DAILY
TELEVISION PROGRAM

Spook Hill Elementary School
321 East North Avenue
Lake Wales, FL 33853
Barbara Waldrop, Library Media Specialist

Impetus for program.

"Spook Hill Live" began as the idea of the library media specialist and the PTO president. The PTO purchased the necessary equipment over a two-year period, and our daily in-school video program began.

Implementation and description.

The program informs the students, faculty, and parents of activities within the school and their community. The video crew of sixth graders is chosen by the teachers from each of the sixth-grade classes. Two students act as camera crew for half the year, as good camera work takes time to develop. Other crew members' jobs are holding cue cards, supplying title cards, acting as announcer and writing out announcements, and putting all materials in order for immediate use.

Synchronizing signs and props is the work of the crew members for the "Spook Hill Live" daily video program. Spook Hill Elementary School, Lake Wales, Florida.

The length of the broadcast is usually five to seven minutes, although the longest show so far ran almost twenty minutes.

During the year, every student in the school has a chance to be on the show. We feel the program is helping to build important skills in the students, such as public speaking and assuming responsibility.

Evaluation of program.

The program has improved communication between the school and the parents. Each day's show is taped and parents are able to take the tapes home to view them.

The program is constantly being assessed through comments from students and teachers and being changed to make the show better. Crew members often also come up with new ideas to try to keep the show interesting.

The only problems that have occurred, other than those that happen with any live broadcast, have been some minor technical mishaps. Replacement and updating of equipment should help to iron out these difficulties.

Each broadcast of "Spook Hill Live" is challenging, exciting, and fun. Each experience teaches something that makes the next show easier and more professional.

9

High School Library Media Center Activities

ALTERNATIVE HIGH SCHOOL ACTIVITIES

Garfield High School (Continuation School)
4487 Oregon Street
San Diego, CA 92116
Stephanie Bass, Library Media Specialist

Impetus for program.

Garfield High School is a small alternative school for students who have not met minimum requirements at regular comprehensive high schools. Learning is accomplished through individual instruction and counseling. The library media center is located in the center of the building and is a central part of this alternative program. We had to decide how to minimize the inconvenience of the design and location while making the library media resources available to the student body.

Implementation and description.

Because the main portion of the building is "open," with the library media center in the middle, the center literally becomes the hub of the school. There are five open classrooms and four enclosed classrooms around it. The enclosed classrooms house a reading lab, a career center, the student-body office, and a computer lab. The open area serves multiple purposes. In addition to serving as the library media center, it functions as the auditorium when there is an assembly. A section of the center serves as a tutoring area for basic skills or second language tutors.

Adjacent to the library media center and connected by open doorways is an all-purpose resource room, with textbook stacks, audiovisual production, and teacher resource areas including computers and duplicating equipment.

The library media center is decorated in orange, gold, and brown. The first general impression on entering the area is one of attractiveness and openness. Large bulletin boards and open-space areas are maintained with displays on current topics.

Basic skills teacher works with students. Garfield High School (Continuation School), San Diego, California.

Evaluation of program.

Although very much the hub of all activity, the open library center concept is not without major problems. Noise and loss of library books have been the two main difficulties and have yet to be resolved.

Teachers in the open classrooms complain bitterly about noise and lack of privacy. When a film is shown in one classroom, it is usually disturbing to another. Most students working in the library media center do not seem to be bothered by the general noise level and the library media specialist has developed a high tolerance for it. Short of putting up walls for all classrooms, no one has come up with a solution to the problem.

The loss of library books is presently being handled in two ways. The Dewey sections that were most often subject to theft were removed from open shelving and put at the circulation desk, where they must be requested by the students. We also purchase books in paperbound form whenever possible, lowering the cost of library media center losses.

We enjoy our library media center and have learned to live with its problems.

DESIGN FEATURES FOR A HIGH SCHOOL LIBRARY MEDIA CENTER

Pine Forest High School
2500 Longleaf Drive
Pensacola, FL 32506
Pat Thorne, Library Media Specialist

Impetus for program.

The original layout of the library media center by the architects was sterile and unimaginative.

Implementation and description.

The area in front of the circulation desk was originally designed as a reference area. The staff desired to have reference and research activities away from traffic and busy circulation activity, so this space was changed to the leisure area for paperbacks, current magazines, fiction books, and short story collections. Also located here are current newspapers, along with casual furniture, rocking chairs, and student art.

The office area can be observed by all patrons because of the glass wall, yet there is a generous work space with murals in selections and colors that add depth and calmness.

The history collection and audiovisual materials are arranged behind the circulation desk behind which is a mural that has a pleasing, soothing effect. Below this is equipment for viewing microforms.

Audiovisual and microform area with mural painted by high school art classes. Pine Forest High School, Pensacola, Florida.

Beyond and adjacent to the history section viewing area is another angular area housing conference rooms and additional viewing equipment. Portraits of our administrators hang between the conference room doors. Pictures and microforms are stored nearby.

To the left, there is a window section with hanging plants. Circulating books have been arranged along the wall and there is counter-height shelving protruding from these walls at complimentary angles.

There is sufficient seating in two areas for class groups to complete individual research with the assistance of the teachers and library media staff.

Magazine indexes are placed near the storage area door of the office. Near this area are encyclopedias, copy machines, and the card catalog.

Each area of the center is identified with carved wood markers constructed by students in the wood shop classes.

Evaluation of program.

No formal evaluation has been completed. Comments from students and faculty are positive. Visitors are amazed at the overall effect of color, student art work, and arrangement of space.

A CAREER ROOM

Sterling Heights High School
12901 Fifteen Mile
Sterling Heights, MI 49245
Iris Evans, Library Media Specialist

Impetus for program.

The Career Room has been functioning for six years. Some of the parent volunteers have been part of the program since its inception. The six student counselors and the student population they serve use the facility as a library resource. The counselors also provide professional advice and recommend materials for purchase.

Implementation and description.

The Career Room in the Sterling Heights High School library is a separate facility within the library media center complex, containing materials for self-evaluation, career exploration, financial aid, current employment markets and futures, résumé and job application materials, and college catalogs.

An overview of the Career Resource Room. Sterling Heights High School, Sterling Heights, Michigan.

Both print and nonprint materials are available. Computers provide practice for standard tests such as the ACT and SAT. Current information about job markets, careers, colleges, schools, and scholarships anywhere in the United States is available on computer. Microfiche readers and printers provide an alternate delivery system.

The Michigan Employability Development Plan (EDP) begins in ninth grade, when students explore careers during a social studies unit. The EDP folders are forwarded from the four feeder junior high schools to Sterling Heights High School each fall. Ten or more volunteer parents, under the direction of the library media specialist, prepare the student files and store the folders in the Career Room.

During the school year, the sophomores are scheduled into the Career Room for a five-day unit by their English teachers. The library media specialist, assisted by the volunteers, continues the EDP program begun in the ninth grade. The activities provide an orientation to the center; teach self-evaluation techniques in the areas of personality, aptitudes, and interests; and continue career exploration. An overview of learning experiences is recorded.

Juniors are scheduled into the Career Room from their English classes to explore sources of scholarships and financial aid. Financial aid applications must be submitted at this time in order to secure the financial aid needed for continuing education after graduation.

Seniors are given two days in the Career Room to update their EDP files and complete a personal educational and employment raw data sheet. The parent volunteers store this information on the computers and place a hard copy in the EDP files.

The graduating student now has a complete educational and employment record that may be used to generate résumés and employment applications. The completed EDP folders are presented to the graduating students as they pick up their caps and gowns. The computer disks are stored and may be updated, with current hard copies made upon request.

Evaluation of program.

The Career Room serves adults in the school community upon request, by phone or in person. Some parents ask for information through their children. The center is open only during school hours.

Bibliography

Graves, B. "Facility Planning: Shedding Light on Learning," *American School and University* 57:7 (March 1985), pp. 88-90.

Hathaway, W. E. "Light Colour and Air Quality: Important Elements of the Learning Environment?" *Education Canada* 27 (Fall 1987), pp. 35-44.

Hathaway, W. E., and D. R. Fielder. "A Window on the Future: A View of Education and Educational Facilities." Columbus, Ohio: Council of Educational Facility Planners, International, September 1986.

Veatch, Julian Lamar. *Library Architecture and Environmental Design: The Application of Selected Environmental Design Factors to the Planning of Public Library Facilities.* Doctoral Thesis. Florida State University, Tallahassee, 1979.

Walsh, W. Bruce. *Theories of Person-Environment Interaction: Implications for the College Student.* Iowa City, Iowa: American College Testing Program, 1973.

Wohlfarth, H. *Color and Light Effects on Students: Achievement, Behavior and Physiology.* Edmonton, Alberta: Planning Services Branch, Alberta Education, 1986.